The Listening

WINNER OF THE 2003 CAVE CANEM POETRY PRIZE
Founded in 1996 by Toi Derricote and Cornelius Eady,
Cave Canem is a workshop/retreat for African American poets
and is dedicated to nurturing and celebrating African American
culture. Cave Canem sponsors a poetry prize for the best
original manuscript by an African American poet who has
not yet been professionally published.

D1040978

The Listening

POEMS BY KYLE DARGAN

The University of Georgia Press   Athens and London

Published by the University of Georgia Press

Athens, Georgia 30602

© 2004 by Kyle Dargan

All rights reserved

Designed by Mindy Basinger Hill

Set in 10.5/15 Minion

The paper in this book meets the guidelines for
permanence and durability of the Committee on
Production Guidelines for Book Longevity of the
Council on Library Resources.

Printed in the United States of America

08 07 06 05 04 P 5 4 3 2 1

Library of Congress Cataloging-in-Publication Data

Dargan, Kyle.

  The listening : poems / by Kyle Dargan.

     p. cm.

  "Winner of the 2003 Cave Canem Poetry Prize."

  ISBN 0-8203-2661-5 (pbk. : alk. paper)

  I. Title.

  PS3604.A74L57 2004

  811'.6—dc22

                              2004001272

British Library Cataloging-in-Publication Data available

For my mother—
whose gift I honor

For "Slim"—
whose beauty inspired a first poem

For Reetika—
who, most importantly, is missed

What music hurts the massive head tonight . . .

WOLE SOYINKA

Contents

Foreword

QUINCY TROUPE

To listen is to hear sounds, human or otherwise: bird calls trilling through spring or summer days; car horns blaring insistently in traffic jams; musical instruments skedaddling through jazz riffs or symphonic flourishes; the wind whooshing breathless through trees when Mother Nature speaks; the pounding of ocean waves, roaring and hissing when they hit rocks or crash ashore; DJ's scratching records on turntables under rhythmic rapper's scats; and on a book's page, and in hushed or throbbing air, a poet's voice moving us (or turning us off) in the way language is crafted and structured in a poem.

In a sense, the listener, or reader, of poems reacts (positively or negatively) to the way rhythm and meter enhance music in poetic lines and to the deep familiarity that the images and metaphors in those lines evoke. All of this, however, depends on the listener's or reader's geographic or educational background, cultural dislikes or likes, and the subjective taste in what makes poetry work or not work for him or her. It's all very interesting how this comes together, this simpatico, the bond that occurs between reader and poet.

This bonding happened for me from the first moment I encountered the manuscript of Kyle Dargan, while judging the contest for the 2003 Cave Canem Poetry Prize. After reading the headings he gave to two of the five sections that break up the book, the first thing I noticed was that he was a neologist. Mr. Dargan named the first section "Chronograffiti" and the second "Chronograffiti (b-sides)." These designations intrigued me with their musical influences. His use of the term "Invocation" to start the book and the neologism "Outvocation" to end the volume further fascinated me. Then I read the opening lines of his manuscript in his "Invocation," titled "Of the Sun" (p. 1), and I was hooked. (I also liked the book's original title "The Tortoise & The Square," though I like the current title very much as well.) Those opening lines were:

> This skin has
> a deeper appetite
> for light than most.

What did he mean by "This skin has / a deeper appetite / for light than most"? I was fascinated, I remember thinking of black or brown skin. Then I read the next several lines, and I was knocked out by the structure and rhythm of them and surprised by the juxtaposition of the images:

> It appears
> dark—on surface
> just milking
>
> rays from a black
> body. The black body that acts
> on browns and tans. The sun's
>
> rhythm resonates
> with the equatorial spine, the
> defining line—blue black, (further up)
>
> brown, (further) high
> yellow. Hierarchy?

These lines evoked for me both the continent of Africa and the history of African Americans in the United States, especially when Dargan concludes this passage with the word "Hierarchy?," posed as a question, because this "Hierarchy" of color is a huge dilemma for many people in both Africa and the United States, even today.

And Dargan ends his poem riffing on this problem with the following lines:

Sunlight, the language

of melanocytes. Diglossic
skin, chromatic kin. Come
together reluctant collage.

I really loved the closure of this poem, what it evoked for me, especially, "Diglossic / skin, chromatic kin. Come / together reluctant collage." I was struck by the use of the words "melanocytes," which means roughly, "cells and pigments in the skin that control melanin," and "Diglossic," which means, "someone who's able to code switch, to speak in two dialects of a language."

African Americans do this every day within the race, when negotiating not only the American language but also the language of our skin, which is a very complex act and is at the very heart of his poem. The color-line dilemma is a deep political and human problem that African Americans (and, indeed, ALL Americans) face in this country every day, and "chromatic kin" is a wonderful image for humankind. Many in this country resist Dargan's last sentence, "Come / together reluctant collage." They resist by refusing to fuse, whether that fusion is in regards to culture, politics, or skin tone and race. How we come together is the core historical question and problem that has always faced our country.

But this poem can be read another way, if we look at the first word in the second line of each stanza from top to bottom. Read this way the poem offers up this reading: "a dark body with yellow skin." Very clever, and it lets us know we are in the company of a crafty, first-rate mind. (The ideas and images in the poem also serve as recurrent metaphors throughout the book.) These lines fit together in a color scheme that spans the entirety of African American skin tones: "The black body that acts / on browns and tans. . . . the / defining line—blue black, (further up) / brown, (further) high / yellow . . . the language / of melanocytes. Diglossic / skin, chromatic kin." When one looks at these images together, they add up to a "reluctant collage."

Besides the obvious political overtones of the poem, the structure of the poem, the attention paid to poetic craft, the way Dargan turns his lines on a dime, what his images evoke, and the music that pulsates through the language are first rate. Which brings me to the title of the book, *The Listening.* Even though I liked the first title, I fully understand and appreciate why he changed it. This new title suggests not only the reader's participation in the aural sound of Dargan's language ("The sun's / rhythm resonates / with the equatorial spine, the / defining line—blue black, (further up) / brown (further) high / yellow. Hierarchy?") but also the poet's voice underneath and behind the music of the lines written here. The poet's heartbeat.

After I found out the name of the poet I had selected for the Cave Canem prize, I got his telephone number, called Mr. Dargan, and asked him a few questions about himself and about poetry. He said he'd write me back, and in his letter he told me that "where a musician's sound doesn't or is not allowed to fully transmit their emotion is where these poems start to dig."

The poem "Redefinition" (p. 6), about East Orange, New Jersey, a place Dargan knows well, because it is very close to where he was born and raised in Newark, is a good example of digging beyond "a musician's sound" to "fully transmit . . . emotion." As in "Of the Sun," the language and images marry to give us a wonderful collage, this time of a place that was once an urban area on the upswing but that has now started a slow decline so that it is presently "less and less of a city, no buildings tall— / three floors at the most but enough stories / to fill every window. It feels like what it is. / Hood," where "most dogs will bite" and "the birds fly away at a glance." Sharp, telling imagery. But there is more. We see "squirrels" that "have adjusted"—like humans—and "One has learned to peer / through the screen door and see who is in our kitchen." The poet says this "deserves something" and breaks off a piece of "cinnamon raisin bread" that he calls a "galaxy"—because of its "swirls and shriveled grapes—orbit lines / and planets"—and tosses "it in the squirrel's direction. She crawls over, / stands up to eat." Once the squirrel is standing upright, the comparison to a human beggar pops into our heads. It is a fresh, unusual analogy. Then the surprise (I love surprises in poetry) closure:

> . . . Then back to four legs,
> combing the ground, only to become biped again—switching
> back and forth as if evolution
> is some LP you can scratch and backspin.

All humans come from animals, and "evolution" is how we all came to stand on two legs. But Dargan mulls over whether our "switching / back and forth" is like "some LP you can scratch and backspin." The image of "scratch and backspin" lets us know this poet locates himself squarely in the hip-hop, rap generation. Dargan wrote to me that he likes "to work from the small moment to the larger social context" and that *The Listening* is mainly a "synthesis that bridges the divide between past tradition and modern riffing—bringing them together to coexist in a space." Where "Hip-hop runs up against jazz, African ancestors stand next to civil rights leaders, the post-9/11 America is juxtaposed with sixties/seventies family portraits and possible futures."

This aforementioned menu is a large order for anyone to deal with, not to mention a very young man. But Dargan is an immensely talented poet, and I am eager to read his future work.

So many poems in this book are exceptional, but I list here a few that merit special attention: "*Satin Touch*," "Search for Robert Hayden," "How Dwayne Got Knocked Out," "Chiaroscuro," "Rock w/ You," "Surrender I: Commission," and "For the Returning." I will allow Mr. Dargan's own voice to close this introduction with a few select lines from his poem titled "Ahboo" (p. 10), which, in its descrip-

tion of a baby's world, does a fitting job of summarizing again some
of the themes raised in the book's opening poem, the "coming to-
gether" of arms, of skin, and earlier in "Ahboo," of lips; the creation
of poetic language; and ultimately the way race and culture can carry
us into a new world:

> All of us who look down to you
> at some point wish we could grab our world
> by the hem of its dress
> and tug until someone takes notice
>
> or until two brown arms
> lower from the sky—reaching
> to lift us up—and carry us for the time
> we need to be carried.

Acknowledgments

Versions of these poems first appeared in the following publications.
African American Review: "6:38 A.M., Mississippi Time"; "Satin Touch"
Black Renaissance/Renaissance Noire: "Redefinition"
Callaloo: "Ahboo"; "1975"; "Melody Forensic"; "Old Ways"
Denver Quarterly: "Of the Sun"; "In the Adjacent Days"
LIT: "Misornithology"
River Styx: "Search for Robert Hayden"
Shenandoah: "Bluff"; "Parcel"
Typo Magazine: "Yin"
"Of the Sun" was featured on *Poetry Daily* (www.poems.com)

I can't say exactly when or how the first seeds of this book were sown, but surely I have many to thank for its fruition—first being all my teachers from kindergarten through high school, especially Mrs. McAdams and Mr. Onion (what we don't realize in America is that those are the years when the true mind is formed, people who really want revolution need to start there); next, my family(ies)—Johnson, Dargan, Williams (I can never say I feel lonely in this world); lastly, my mentors and friends—Lisa Russ Spaar (I might have ignored writing if it had not been for your class and then your support), Rita Dove, Charles Wright, Kyle Thompson (for instilling how serious poetry *is,* not can be), Conor Quinlan (for antics++), Reetika Vazirani (for honesty), Charles Rowell (we'll have to see about cutting that album one day), Natasha Trethevey, David Wojahn, and Kevin Young, and, of course, one time for Jersey (we're still doing it).

+ + +

Of the Sun

This skin has
a deeper appetite
        for light than most.

It appears
dark—on surface,
        just milking

rays from a black
body. The black body that acts
        on browns and tans. The sun's

rhythm resonates
with the equatorial spine, the
        defining line—blue black, (further up)

brown, (further) high
yellow. Hierarchy?
        Sunlight, the language

of melanocytes. Diglossic
skin, chromatic kin. Come
        together reluctant collage.

Chronograffiti

Search for Robert Hayden

The garage has not been allowed to breathe
for months now. The smell of moving,
uprooting, cures in the arid Texas heat—
scents not to be romanticized but handled
carefully so that no boxes topple.
We are looking for "The Middle Passage,"
first we must clear a walking path.
Books yelp like kennel pups through holes in their crates,
books that are no longer books
but subheads in chimeras of collected poems.
Next, Copacetic Victims of the Latest Dance Craze—
all originals bearing signatures
like birth certificates. Clifton, no gray.
Komunyakaa, w/ beard. Eady,
looking young as the lost member of New Edition.
Most out of print, and born before I was pressed
in flesh. The past presented, Hayden is still hiding somewhere.
Putting an ear to the walls doesn't help, this year-old house
barely knows its own nooks and stashes.
Hell, round them all up—in minutes
we'll be standing knee deep in
the unselected poems of black literature.
This is how we will find him:
on our hands and knees,
combing over flailed books—seashells
beneath a forgotten tide.
Occasionally we'll wrench something up,
not what we are looking for, and read it anyway.

Redefinition

EAST ORANGE, N.J.

Less and less of a city, no buildings tall—
three floors at the most but enough stories
to fill every window. It feels like what it is.
Hood: most dogs will bite,
the birds fly away at a glance. These squirrels, though,
have adjusted. One has learned to peer
through the screen door and see who is in our kitchen.
That deserves something. No cashews
in the cabinet, cinnamon raisin bread will do.
The swirls and shriveled grapes—orbit lines
and planets. I break off a piece of this galaxy,
tossing it in the squirrel's direction. She crawls over,
stands up to eat. Then back to four legs,
combing the ground, only to become biped again—switching
back and forth as if evolution
is some LP you can scratch and backspin.

Last Dragons

After-dinner ninjas * In the backyard,
me and my brother roundhousing
and backhanding lightning bugs
into a dim oblivion *

Every strike accented by polyoctave screams
and pained Bruce Leroy expressions * An hour into it
our hands begin to glow like my hero's
fists in *The Last Dragon* * We move our arms

in those unlocking circles—bodies
quickened with the power
to shatter exoskeletons
like stacks of flame-glazed bricks *

"Who's the master?" * We'd wait for Sho'nuff,
shogun of Harlem, so we could raise our neon fingers

and answer, "I am" *

Satin Touch

The younger of two brothers runs around the shop,
actively resisting female influence. I sit

next to their mother in the cafeteria-style chair beside the sofa.
The lone white hairdresser is pregnant, the air heavy

with woman talk. "You all stomach, Myrt, you having
a boy. When you have a girl, you get stomach, legs, tail,

ereythang." The other two girls finish their folk diagnosis
and proceed to share their own childbearing tales—

one for each baby picture logged in corners of mirror frames.
After the implicit hour wait, one calls me over.

They know I'm a university kid—book in hand, twangless speech
but slang enough to gain trust. She says something about

my Indian hair. I think *slave master* and say nothing.
The mass of hair on my head, a batch of history, a spectacle. "Yeah,

I wanna see Bird's cornrows" one girl sasses as they crowd around.
She takes the challenge, blow-drying and greasing my scalp,

resting her breasts on my shoulders while she gets the part
straight. The motherly work of her hands

jostles my head between heaven and hell. Each pull and tuck
burning, each brush of flesh soothes. She braids,

we talk, forgetting our audience until she snaps
on black rubber bands and hands me a mirror: $15 is the damage.

I give her twenty, stare deeply as a carnal tension
unhinges. The shop bubbles with naughty giggles—

suds and sass trailing my path out the busted screen door.

Ahboo

FOR LITTLE JEHAN

Glottal, bilabial, mostly
monosyllabic—you speak the same tongue
as Carlos Williams's sea-elephant,
the exquisite gibberish that is poetry.

Sometimes, high pitched like dolphin talk.
I wonder, if you sang off San Juan's bay
would the porpoises understand
and spout saltwater in agreement.

What you do not say is clearest.
Your face is a satellite,
sending crisp signals to receiving eyes,
fluent in the ethereal language of minds.

And the message is ever changing.
Your world is a cliff—
always on the brink of plummeting
into laughter, tears,

forehead rippling confusion.
But there is always a pair of legs
to run toward and embrace. For that,
your life we envy.

All of us who look down to you
at some point wish we could grab our world
by the hem of its dress
and tug until someone takes notice

or until two brown arms
lower from the sky—reaching
to lift us up—and carry us for the time
we need to be carried.

Halfway House

*No one knows about that day or hour, not even the angels in
heaven, nor the Son, but only the Father. As it was in the days
of Noah, so it will be at the coming of the Son of Man.*
—Matthew 24:36–37

He needed a place to stay before
the second coming, a space for rest and re-

acclamation. Still, it's been six days now.
Every morning I get up, and he's

at my kitchen table doing the crossword
puzzle in ink. There's a twitch in his eye

when I turn on the stove. No butter,
he eats the grits but never touches

the porgies—fillets waste away while
he sinks in his chair, stares out

the window. He's flesh again. On his shoulders
dead metaphors quicken, the weight of the world

alive around him. To question the father is to question
himself, and the last thing a point man needs

is doubt. This morning his pillowcase
is red with sweat. No paper this morning,

he's on the balcony, waiting for his ride.
As a nimbus begins to threaten the dawn, I think

"remember, no water, fire this time"—
the world re-members through fire this time.

Single-Ride

"Brother, brother" a man
calls me in a language left
to monolithic hair and revolt.
It's become hustle-talk
like *say brother,*
I'm just trying to eat or
hey brother, got some nice sunglasses
here—five dollars. My own
brother calls me pisan or nigga,
but this man rooted next to the turnstile
says "come on, I got you"—
pointing at an entry for downtown
C and E. I watched him get three "sisters"
through for free. His trick—
take a dead single-ride Metrocard,
rub the magnetic strip with a furious thumb
until the paper warms. The skin
and electrons he strips from his body
make the gate sing
when the card swipes. "Go 'head." I move
slow, unsure why this ride is free.
Is this man one of many
the MTA laid off—repaying the favor
one dollar and fifty cents at a time?
Or is this skin—a reparation
offered only to those also sprouted
from seeds watered with fire hoses?
I want to say "good looking out
brother" as my pelvis pushes
against the metal bar. Instead I nod my head up,
meaning to say thank you in my language
trained to disbelieve simple kindness.

This Knight

Because you are for me
        what that phantom piece of shrapnel was for you—
        slicing your myth from the Korean war
        to sit back on the heartland's stone bench.
Because I have three years in Bloomington
        while you did eight in Indiana State
        Pen—robbery.
Because no matter how much I show,
        don't tell, who will see this?
Because the "Hard Rock" that eroded in your story
        has his own cell in my sleep.
        When I go to look, he reaches between bars,
        grabs my arms—his thumb pressing the bone
        as if it is a doorbell.
Because farm children smirk
        as I teach "Belly Song." *And I, and I . . .*
Because the streets of circle city mutter
        "some nights, Etheridge chose to lay with us."

Dementia

Red, blue. Black
through cereal box 3-D
glasses. Dark: no streetlight
on our block. Nothing seen
beyond the negative horizon of the sidewalk.
I see my father rising up
the lawn. Not liquored. I'm glad.
Not like the time he was a crying statue
on the curb, and I asked him—"Are you
a man or a mouse"—the best I could do
at seven.

Soon I'll go back and forth,
trophy for a two-man team.
This Friday he wants to take me
on a ride. Opening the door
so he can't ring the bell—the sound of it
says too much—I survey him,
my backpack readied, vision coded
red and blue to see the ghouls
swimming in the dark.

Mom thinks they will hurt
my eyes. Dad is a DAD: lets boys play.
He lobbies for fire-'n'-ice
tinted lenses, grows meaner
as they argue—my glasses homespun
catalyze. When he storms out
under a clear sky, things change.

Life Equation

My daddy was a bass line, and mom
an anthology of Newark nights—
her arm a high-rise poem
he would run his baritone blue cipher over,
over and over again.
They loved in translation, grew apart,
grew to love me from different homes—
leaving me an adulteration of the blues,
of the absence and question they live.

How Dwayne Got Knocked Out

MONTCLAIR, N.J.

We were running on the break, 2 on 1,
and the ace didn't see Dwayne coming
fierce on the left. I laid the ball down
like a spade—ferociously sweet
don't-look pass. Dwayne skyed on Kobe,
left his prints on the backboard.
We up, 6-5, game 11.

Two jokers, they shouted
friendly shit talk, all the way down the court.
Sounded like something about Dwayne's mama,
then something concerning
the midair intimacy of Dwayne's balls
to Kobe's mouth—the hot blacktop
soaking it all up.

At 8-9 Kobe posted up on Dwayne,
gave him an old-school bump
and tear-dropped one in the netless rim.
For punctuation Kobe
placed the ball in Dwayne's chest.
Dwayne then grazed his knuckle hair
on Kobe's eyelash (D's brother
posted under hoop,

letting the lesson go unabridged).
The two scrapped—
missed fists flew like shrapnel. Kobe's big.
Dwayne ran / stole
a stickball bat, came back / made it a kendo staff.
Another fast break, three-man
weaving—Sean tried to stop Dwayne,
tried to dodge Dwayne's, tried to get Kobe
out of the way,

        but he kept carving air
until the stick broke. Kobe's big.
Dwayne ran, plucked an Olde English bottle
from a bruised-up trash can. His pitch missed. Kobe
pissed, picked up Dwayne, punched
his temple hard enough to open
an old suture in the cave of his mouth.
Two teeth, stalactites, dropped hard
like last dominos in a hand.
Kobe cast an Ali-shadow.
Dwayne dazed—eyes flashed
red and blue, bleeding in dimensions.
The small stickball kids had called
the cops—red/blue for real.
We were running.

*Early nineties urban slang for no-name sneakers

I figured mine was Reebok game,
and let the Foot Locker zebra fit me
for a pair of Pumps®
while Mom was off lost in bins of socks.

My thumb sunk into the orange bubble on the tongue
eight times, until the space around my foot
hugged like a blood-pressure band—it was the shoe
that swelled before you cooked somebody on the court.
No was all my mother said.

Driving home bagless, she told me
Reebok supports apartheid in South Africa.
The oracles at the barbershop,
brilliant in windbreaker suits,
said it was like segregation.
But how could people say NO COLOREDS
when *African* is nothing but?

Larry Johnson, he wore Reeboks—
turquoise thunder poster-dunking with his
hair   part and
tooth   gap all synchronized.
Even his endorsement alter ego, Grandmama™,
wore the sneaks with her classiest Sunday dress.

My mother wouldn't bend. She found fortitude
in the fact that I didn't understand.
I was a Knicks fan, damn sure
wasn't going to run around in Jordans®.

We agreed on a bootleg pair of Ewings,
and I had to dribble the ball heavier
to drown out the kids shouting "Aaahh-ha's"*
from porches as I walked to the park.

nap · i · ness

When kinks began clustering on my head,
cousins named them naps.
I had to adapt—forget them
and learn to love the Brillo.
It was like wool. I
was like Jesus, Julius, Malcolm,
Amiri—unkempt and proud.
In came hip-hop, and the barber sheared my hair
in the shape of the Ka'bbah: black-box history,
our chronicle recorded forever inside.

But I learned someone had edited
my text with different blood
than it was fashioned in—
loosening the pages like lye
so the words wouldn't twist or dreadlock.
Then I realized
I was never truly in *his* likeness
nor the doctor's
nor the prophet's
nor the poet's. I am enigma—
living one history, combing another.

On Men

What a shave does for a man—opening

his profile, redefining
the boundaries like a treaty
between follicle and flesh.
We expect the politics of faces
to be steadfast.

The chameleon cream
hisses out the cylinder, a viscous jade
expanding into white.
Three stacked blades uncover what was
blurred by weekend's sfumato.

As my stepfather shaves off the beard
he's toted since he left
the shag Vietnamese fields
thirty-five years ago, I know
there's some revolution within him.

Planting his body before the mirror,
he strips the hair down to an island
above his lip—I can only imagine
the things he is forgetting, fields
clearing in his mind.

Surrender ɪɪ: Chop

Her impression:

carved stories out of balsam,
placed the shaving in my palm,

               soaked in indigo,
               the night-owl's blood,
and rolled
against the fallows of my days.
I was intrigued,
then the ink dried.

The Battlefield

FOR DARRELL BURTON

That night a mantle of snow fell over all the bodies, sharp
and fine like sky grating itself. Limbs twice brittle, cold on
corpus morta, sunk while ground and horizon grew
to touch each other. Five months, the icy shards fell like one name,
cataloging every breathless man as one casualty. It dissolved
with their flesh and seeped into the pores beneath the grass.

Widows flocked to the wells, to the rivers—scooping hands and buckets,
shoes and skirt bottoms. Each poured what they gathered
into wooden bowls, flexed forearms with the alchemy of making
dough they'd feed to pear-shaped kilns. When the bread had baked,
they gathered all the daughters, made them watch while the boys ate.

Surrender III: Study

Relief sculpture on her skin entitled "childhood"—
empires preserved with cocoa butter
not dry cavern air. My fingers catch
the shallow divots in her rear. *There?*
I ask, and learn a story of hips
infected, a search that left proof
but found nothing. I tongue a mark
on her stomach. *And here?*—a newborn,
a glass lung, three months, the electrodes
took pieces. I kiss these places,
opening pores like causeways. Tonight
we will lay down and sweat within.
The rogue spirit taking asylum
in her body, tonight we'll flush it out.

6:38 A.M., Mississippi Time

(MYRLIE EVERS TO MEDGAR EVERS)

Sun's light blind-sliced
and spliced on your broad nose,
I get up early to watch

your face bathe in this tasteless glaze.
I know it has to end. Soon
I'll be downstairs, boiling and whisking,

and you, Medgar, will be gone—stealing away
into the dark Mississippi tide.
Sometimes I wake up and wonder

what's a movement to me . . . I
like the selfish static of me and you, comforter
impermeable, the way you say *Myrlie*

as if it is the color you'd paint
all refuge. What else is there,
except that world waiting for you

on the doorstep? But it's not here,
in our mornings where your eyes are deep
and brown as a mystery.

Second Sky

1. The Pre-land

We were chattel, effortlessly
hemmed, the air so heavy
and numbing in that place.

We were made to mine
the planet, allowed to keep
what suited us (with no use for currency,
most affixed their gains
to their irons, until they forgot
what they were).

              Bred in the dark-
Darwinism of that place, slowly
we built immunity to irony.

Those vulnerable survived
no longer than three moons.

Those vaguely stricken lost their voices—
tongues ossified and became runes.

ii. Shard

During the years now torn
from our spines, planets came
thus—born splinter, born sac
pinched off the curve of another pastel body.
We believe the oldest stars
still show where their loss
never healed. For us
a higher spirit has deemed
gore, or fusion: our children are
the cut and the blood and the ochre
dusk besetting the edges of our daily
wound. We won't claim
tragedy, for the triptych
folds into flight. Their bodies,
young, scar over dark and stealth
as this medium we are peddled through.
We warn them *do not open your mouth,*
that *this is not water.* Empty carafes,
we christen them with breath
and sail each one into the crisp bleakness,
knowing they will float—
denser than nothing in our world.

iii. Fable

Exodus casts these roles:
you the princess, I the scribe. Your suitor
the prince of the tribe across the river.
I wait for the waters to bleed
over the banks and cultivate my words—
my mood rising orange as the owl's eye.

You keep me up nights,
my hands dragging the rest of me
to the garden just to touch.
I'm offered, despite your mother's
warning not to take my hands—
they've been known to burn, and
I love the sandalwood in you.

Together we are incense—a smoky ponytail
the prince follows to where we hide.
My death is at your hand,
the sweetest ending we know.
Drawing the curtains of eyes
my face bows down toward yours,
        fading negative, only to wake as a child
on the river—the bank soil soft
beneath, you a vista across the water,
smiling, my cue.

IV. Orbit

Where were you during the eclipse?
I was hiding with the sun.

Was the moon sweating?
No, but because it was dark enough we wept.

Did you get to puppeteer the sea?
Our hands were too large   I tried to regress.

But there, you were . . . ?
Nothing, searching out an emerald—a distraction.

What was Diana wearing?
A green headdress, a rune necklace.

What was her answer?
(His thumb on the dusky braille of her nipple) Yes.

v. The Truth

Within the village, we left the openings
of our shacks unsheathed, offering
free passage so it could roam
among us—none dared tame it.
As we slept, it would come
to sniff at our wiry shadows, nibble our toes.
Some people it swallowed whole
and when the morning came,
we'd say night happened to them.

What myth we knew of it
we transcribed in leaf mosaics
on our children's walls.
No one ever put eyes on it, assumed
it was some aching
behemoth with rows of teeth
infinite as ripples on a pond.
But one day, eve of the king's death,
we saw it, small enough—crawling
into the prince's ear, its footprints
fossilizing as it moved.

Fingers, Fader

When they reminisce over you, listen.
—C. L. Smooth

Melody Forensic

If somebody told me I had only one hour to live,
I'd spend it choking a white man. I'd do it nice and slow.
—Miles Davis

Years in the gristle of knuckles. Thick muscle
at the palm's base. Fingers squeezing,
digging valve keys to mold exhales. Some pain
pinched by the mouthpiece—would it wail
if you had found a pink neck before lead-pipe brass?
Forgive the epigraph. Don't apologize—
your music may taste funny to someone
after reading this. But damn Miles (if I can call you
Miles), why do black men have to scream in art?
What wants off our tongue floats
in the same ether lungs feed metal
(now you got me doing it). Listen,
if "I hurt" falls deaf on their ears,
Kind of Blue is no different.
The black sound congeals in mason jars
lined across the tops of rickety stoves.
We been frying our story, overseasoned
with silences. Miles (I'm calling
you Miles), you don't want to play. Sweet indulgence—
let's pretend we're back at the Five Spot, this poem
just another stage light, move it.
Put the trumpet down. Where would you start?
Maybe there, Mr. Cool at the bar—head lolling,
eyes wilted from your blow,
a coil of saliva in his throat so
sure he can swallow your blue note whole.

Chiaroscuro

Black and white stills of old brass blowers
make a frieze above refrigerated rows
of chardonnays and microbrews.
They play jazz here,
this small C'ville sandwich shop
where the kick-
snare-bass always sets the air bumpin'
like aurora borealis. On the back wall,
there's that picture of Ella
gutting and stretching a note
while Duke Ellington and Benny Goodman
sit front-table center: *DOWNBEAT·*

NYC·1949.
Duke's lips curve with rapture,
while Benny's cool
as the glass of rum in his hand.
Ella's on a reconnaissance mission
in heaven—eyes closed,
translating things we can't see into song.
The strong stage light grows behind her, a halo
premature yet well put.

I remember the week she passed,
WBGO played her tribute for three days.
Mingled within the standards and recorded
reminisces, a song from a live show in Germany
where she freestyled with crickets
stubbornly singing backup. For two days Ella blew
like a nor'easter in June, filling corner offices,
kitchens, and car interiors with sweet sickness.

She's framed here, black with white—
taking subconscious requests
from patrons cycling in and out the shop.
When you leave she remains,
blowing, doin' it to death.

Misornithology

Barber hands move like hummingbirds,
refining my abstract 'fro.
Bergen Street, Newark. Of course,
he's talking jazz while snipping—
all the older scissorsmiths
being avid squint-faced toe tappers.
His words, little talons,
lindy-hop off the tongue.
--Who you like youngblood?
--Byrd.
--Bird was bad man. Sad, but bad.
--What you mean *was*?
--Bird's dead man, been dead.
--Trumpet Byrd?
--Dead Bird.
--Donald Byrd?
--Who? No boy, Charlie—Chan man, Parker.
He motions toward the radio. We bridge
and listen for plumage.

Rock w/ You

A wet forecast in my mother's body,
I am a wick
awaiting the flames of color
pulsing in stereo.
From my standpoint, you are sound—
a flawless low falsetto.
Outside you are young,
chestnut toned, and nimble.

Don't try to fight it. You urge
my parents to dip and spin across
old parquet. I wean from my mother's inertia
the way you'll tiptoe
over fluorescent sidewalks—a new savior
on water, netting converts
with the promise of a lunar walk
on earth. 1980, and there's no need

to speak the stories of Joseph.
No doubting whether there's Gary,
Indiana left in your nose.
No games of rock-skin-glove
(what beats what) or wondering
why a grown man would desire
a small version of himself
covered with fur.

These years are dress rehearsal
for your prime/parabola. America
loves you like a newborn nebula,

pushes toward Earth's outer shell.
Quincy Jones builds you
another shuttle—sturdier beats
for extended flight. Zero G, only you
wonder when the father pawns the son's youth,
how far must he search as a man
to rebody the boy? You answer
with a dance that moves forward
without taking eyes off your wake.

[Murk 'n' Teal Izm]

It's driving him away, the infamous
undefined—

       what ghosts of men call the system.
This is my roommate's last night

at school, off to California. But he'll reach a new high
before the Greyhound beckons. Looking

into his eyes, a cloudy rouge
tinge like massacre water,

we have our first, possibly last,
nonsex related dialogue. He does not want

a B.A. to have to bend over or work his way up.
I don't blame him—"paying dues" is an endangered metaphor.

The starry-striped dreams will cost us:
two-pence dignity,

       eight-pence essence.
He blinks, the mood changes.

"I just wanna start a revolution" he says. It isn't
the weed talking anymore. I tell him I'm rewriting

Gil
Scott-

Heron. He nods and puts his bags in
the belly of the silver carriage. We pound fists—

our hands rough as match heads. "'Til next time,"
until the smoke clears.

(Black) Jack Johnson
or Ghetto Rock and Roll

"Elvis Presley ain't got no soul"
[blasphemy]

"John Coltrane is rock and roll"
[blasphemy]

"You may dig on the Rolling Stones
but they ain't come up with that shyt on they own"
[. . .]

So you're digging up Fish Bone
and Bad Brains, assembling
an exquisite corpse of Afro-rock
attempting to redefine fusion—unplugging
amps from turntables
to tap into a guitar's electric war cry.

It's dope, not that two chord,
straight from the garage to MTV sound,
or the blue-chip rap
that is indentured to sampled tracks.

Have you asked yourself
who this is for.

The mainstream-indie crowd will buy in.

But what of BET—the source
for hip-hoppers visual/musical knowledge?
They know you as Mos Def the emcee,
want Mos Def the emcee
or Mos Def hosting *Def Poetry* on HBO.

Mos Def
as the right arm of JACK JOHNSON,

                    they'll never see it coming.

Maybe it will knock the snot out of hip-hop.
If it flops, the MCA execs will say
you should go back to being black
on both sides—deaf
to the fact that you never faded.

One's for the money

two never shows.
Three has to play the upright,
give the rhythm section a soul.

One revives a tune—
two defibrillator hands pressed to the song's
chest, chanting *check* in threes. No

one can tell the melody is jerry-rigged.
The two soundmen pound
the stage, three minutes 'til

curtains. One shadowy brother says
he can play the drums. Toss him two
drumsticks, he makes fire—third-degree

funk, 1000 B.C. neolithic noise, something
like that. The stage's eyelid rises: twin mic stands |
voluptuous bass | drum set in lotus position. Triangular vibe.

Any anxiousness washes away
with one wave of applause. The drums roll in.
The upright sings steady from its gut

and the DJ, scratching, turns speakers into banshees.
Three sets, sweaty, one last drum solo
and the house is sold. Asked later, they'll say

organichiphopjazz. One picks up the money.
Two never showed. Three full pockets,
fuller futures hit the road.

—FOR THE LEGENDARY FIFTH DYNASTY CREW

Letter: Muddy Waters to Michael S. Harper

I am a ~~black~~ man.   Don't [it] hurt
me—a black ~~man~~ [sharecropper].

      I am a [rolling ~~stone] black~~ man.

We are here, forwarding
address: Maxwell Street market, west Chicago—
soul saving, eight to twelve each night.

I am a ~~black man~~
[lawd-call].
Storefront Sabbaths through Blue Mondays.
O, sweet "I am who am."

Who am I? Some call
me Mud . . . don't matter.
I manned a crop tractor—
say I'm Rolling Fork.

My first wife was the wind,
done left.   So I hopped
      a Pullman to Illinois.

I write because you,
black man, will one day know
the markup on blues.

They may try to short me.

Enclosed is an invoice—
but make them pay what you feel.

Rememory

Bluff

Brownie and Grandma whisper about it in bed—
words large and prickly
as peach pits on their tongues. They cling,
anxious of their own decision.

"The regimen will do him good." My father
seems delinquent enough for military school

in Brownie's eyes. The cruising, uninspired
schoolwork, and dirty room—he'd dealt himself

a tough hand, unwittingly sassing back to Newark's
south ward in his head *hit me, hit me.*
But sometimes it's easier to beat the city
than to beat the house. When Brownie showed

his hand, everyone on Custer Avenue
knew who'd be packing up from the table.

Parcel

Brownie's hands vice around the steering wheel.
Radio stations shift with state lines. Migratory
Thunderbirds and Skylarks are flocking I-95,
families en route to bloodlands.

One is being pushed from this nest—not to learn
flight, but be reminded of its privilege.

Founded for colored boys, integrated to stay afloat,
St. Emma's will polish him with slow, deliberate strokes.

"Just ask for directions, Brownie"—their second circle
through the 495 beltway. A road that travels south,
west, north, then east goes nowhere. But stubborn
will gets them into Virginia. They leave my father on the hill.

He moves from tree to tree—not to be caught
watching them drive off without glancing back.

Inventory

As day-shift expeditor, Brownie shepherds plane parts
through assembly stations. Every piece he knows
by serial—able to navigate the numbered shelves of General Brass
like an old archivist. Though he knows where his son is,

he cannot move him. The way St. Emma's builds boys
there are no pieces—given a mahogany trunk,

they carve warrior's oval eyes, arrowhead chin,
and mantis limbs. The whole—part man, part pestle.

Two days since they carried my father down south,
Brownie takes to the road on his lunch break. The door
opening at noon startles my grandmother—she turns
to see tears leaking from the toughest stone she knows.

"We sent him away" Brownie mutters out his pinched throat.
Uprooted, they fall in and bank against each other.

Elementary

My father calls home to offer Brownie weekly salve
and speak hoarded truth to my grandmother. Sparse
on details, all refrain. "I don't like it, can I come home?"
She reminds him of the money—uniforms, equipment, boots.

It's lost on him, having never asked the investment
be made. "Half a term," she promises, "then we'll see."

At winter break, they plan a visit and breeze south—
sure of direction, bearing cobbler and remorse.

Seeing him, he's still their boy—same except for bruises
and a black eye "from falling during exercises."
Though grandma is a detective, forced to be elite—
black, female, a dual first for Newark police

—this needs no sleuth. With cinched mitts, Brownie deciphers
a stretch of welts too shallow to be tough love.

Nine Winters

February, my father comes home mannish,
feline clean. He doesn't need to be barked at
about chores or school—too relieved to relate
what went down at St. Emma's. His skin is carbon paper,

accounts peeled away and discarded while beneath
impressions keep legible to his eyes only.

Further polarized, father and son share even less—
dinnertime updates, talk of college at best. The stalemate

lasts deep into my father's second youth, until cancer
settles between Brownie's ribs. My father
learns the last lesson of manhood, pathos—attending
his father's side for the long string of final days.

The grave wants all forgiven, and Brownie dissipates
in 1979. I am born soon after, too late.

Chronograffiti (B-sides)

1975

Slouching,
strung out on rope-a-dope,
the vulnerability
shows early. From over the lip
of his trunks the black waist-guard pokes,
exposed like the entrails of an automaton.

Muhammad man-titan, fueled
by precision and diesel
ego, versus the man
he called a beast. So ugly—
fueled by instinct,
too dumb
to appreciate the combinations
unlocking the purples
beneath his skin, too dumb
to realize he should be hurt,
too stubborn
for Frazier to be just a star
in some greater constellation.

Combustion

FOR TIMOTHY THOMAS . . . FOR US

I. FLIGHT (4/7/01)

Don't run, black flame / it will only make you stronger.
                              / all that's needed is one spark.

Ducking around buildings scattered
on concrete like puzzle pieces, you stumble—
your feet knocking like flints. Don't get up. Black flame,

let them lay on hands   you   reach terminal velocity,
the wind no longer fueling your steps. An arm blue
as unspilled blood explodes—crashing

through your back to splinter lungs.
What took forty-one in New York
now only takes 1.

II. FIGHT (4/8/01–4/12/01)

We are rioting for you, black flame—
barricading the streets with burning
couches like the French, though far
from revolutionary. We loot
as if we could steal back enough
to pay for your life. Your killer will pay
with training—forty hours relearning
the spectrum of innocence.

Walking armories, faceless
as the alley of your demise,
now sentinel the streets of Cincinnati.
The mayor has upped the ante—9:00 curfew.
"The violence must stop," he says. The violence
must stop we say. We grow thick
with the thought of that metal leech
lodged within your body.
Seven-hundred clasped cuffs later, we stand
unarmed. They tell us that if we don't go
inside, they will be forced to fire.
More tear gas, white canisters
mining at what little we have left.

III. HOMEGOING (4/14/01)
We are gathered here today
to negotiate with god, to surrender
ourselves. Dressing your corpse in a suit,
we return the earth's porous lantern while you

shimmer away
on the tide of a mother's erosive cries.
As one, the church decides to farm peace
on this plot of death you leave us. On leaving

this place of mourning, this hope refinery,
a police car sprays soft rounds—giving
bruises to match the ones inside.
The flashing chariot pulls off, glowing

like the Nike of Samothrace—streams of blue
light, flapping wings. Victory
flies with them, her head and heart
we plant along with you.

Letting

There was no time for socks
this morning. I shed boots, bend down to see
what hours of burning translate into
visually: skin rubbed shiny—gems
embedded in the balls of ankles.
In three days, flesh, like fantasy,
turns gems scabs, plasma partitions
to protect me from myself.
But as night compiles hours,
I'm tempted to break my own seals
to stay awake. My foot perched stone-still,
blood beads into a mark of affluence,
of wealth self-generated. A drop
falls toward the floor—a marble,
a Mars, a red so bottomless
no wonder our earliest healers
felt a deep draught of this
could fill the body back to living.

On Men

Daddy's hands were one crease
from seamless by the time I was ten—
blank palms kneading into me myth
that every time man touched woman
some of his time lines and grooves dissolved.

When the years begged his erasure
from the old construction-
paper family portraits, I started believing
one of man's side quests
is to be able to present hands
sanded down by loves before they turn
cold—folded over a flesh shell.
The remains to be a cool, smooth brother.

On Men

Start off with what your father drank—
gin with a side of water, coconut rum
and Coke, something hard
with something
to take the teeth out of it.

Two-syllable liquor,
nothing more.
Nothing loquacious,
a drink you could request
without having to take
a breath.

Whatever you choose,
learn to request it—practice
saying *Lemme get a . . .*
in a soaked mahogany voice,
firm yet fluid enough to bend
around the back of a woman's neck
and tug gently at her ear.

Make a quiet event of it.
Hold each sip at the bottom
of your mouth—pressing
slick underside of tongue
against the body of liquid—and

swallow. Look to see
if she is watching.
If she pleases, wait one song
and then find her
orange sweater.
Say it, like your father did.
Bartender, one for the lady
on the opposite shore.

Surrender 1: Commission

Writing you is like skinny dipping
a pond of algaeed language. That squish
my foot sinks in,
everyone has named. I'm not one
for labels—I feel it between my toes and
run on water's back to shore.

—————

In summer camp, braving the lake
on dare, my foot finds a pot
full-nelsoned by the sandy floor.
Excavated, I give it, with my story,
to the counselor. The next morning
it bubbles with grits—
I watch the other children eat.

—————

Here, these fished words.
You heat something up, I promise
to taste it.

Palinode

(*Write* it!)
—Elizabeth Bishop

I found out what cold is
that semester in a physics class.
Actually, it doesn't exist;
the feeling is the loss of heat.

There is no *cold*—
the floor is never cold.
It simply draws from the warmth
welled in our bared feet,
and we feel it.

You aren't cold—
your presence siphons what it wills
from my lungs, my vessels,
my resolve. I write,
wincing. I feel it, though
you do exist.

Writing under the Influence
of *Dirty Havana Trilogy* by Pedro Juan Gutiérrez

Today is growing into its length.
My circadian peak rolls up
alongside my bed like La Niña,
cold, precipitous.
The notebook's open. What
to write? The walls haven't said shit
and Sundays aren't much for material lately:
two condoms on the nightstand
mocking me as usual.
Maybe if I thought less about a first line
and more about sex, I'd have a first line.

Maybe I'll write one of those Love Jones poems,
loquacious yet sexy—two doves, one stone.

So this is what it's come to,

                poems

                        like pebbles
to toss at abandoned tenements.
I'll paint windows on plywood
and tack them over the broken panes,
just like the ones back home.
And afterward—standing outside,
admiring the work—I'll grab
the first derelict thought
that comes through my mind.
When asked for a dollar,
I'll just turn
toward the boarded-up facade and say,
"You see that? That's me."

Surrender IV: Muse

Under the stars, plastic stick 'ems
on the ceiling, we would blaze each other.
Crevices and crooks in the covers, valleys

where the runoff desire from our bodies
would collect. Your mom and pop asleep
upstairs, your sister dreaming

a door over, your bed the lone plateau
in your room's landscape.
We'd lie on top like giants.

Silence was the tongue of that land. That's why
the cat could stay—she was fluently deaf.
I can remember drawing my warm arm

across your chest, you reaching back
and grasping me by the base saying "I know" and
no at the same time. That dry heat giving way

to the view of the distant radiator between the pillars
of your legs. That was years ago,
December. Still sometimes I sit outside,

eyes mapping this foreign Appalachian sky,
waiting for the stars to glow green.

Yin

CHARLOTTESVILLE, VA.

Glinting stones,
offspring of boulder and gust,
dictate my steps
between the train tracks.

Looking up, I catch the mountains
glowing beneath their blue skin—embers
glazed in atmosphere.

At the intersection, orphan iron segments
lay lifeless on the ground,

orange and poisoned by oxygen.

I pause for the landscape
of the phantom artist.

What shall we call this peace?

Surrender v: Revue

When you changed
in front of me
as though I wasn't there,
the boy within said *laugh*—
this is a trick to brew longing. I watched
you, rolled in a towel—
like some hors d'oeuvre,
the man in me said.
I listened as you raked through hair—long
since we were children,
now a measure of distance
between us, the poet
in me said. No voice was right.
You turned away, letting the wall
reverb your breathing
to me—turned as if the water
stilled on your shoulders
was a tongue I spoke
but could no longer read.

Metro Wet

      Attentive reeds grub
deep for clay—thirsty roots
communing with your marrow.

Remember the Meadowlands
as swamps—as substance contented
in flux between fluid and firm.

A month of rain:
Nefertiti-necked fowl
now chorus while we damn
the swollen sky. You glisten,

aloof to the coarse island
(its grumpy silhouette),
and feel the river between swell.
Though we forget
Liberty wades in your tide,

remember why we grafted
bridges over your green—
that spongy land
bent on being built around.

Letter to an American Cousin

Uncle Sam is just one big bruise, cousin
—schizo, self-mutilating. Keeps breaking
the same ribs, thinking
it's someone else he's swinging at.
You inheriting his dreams, kicking
and twitching in bed,
suffocating under sheets—
every cover, twenty feet of water.
Your mother has to shake him,
say *you dreaming Sam*
(carefully) *you dreaming* (remembering the time
one of his flailing arms
left a nightmare beneath her eye).

Didn't he swear off his morning beer
that day he got up to shave
and the mirror / his reflection / his face / complexion
kept click-switching like the View-Master
you haven't played with since you were seven.
He can't show you, but he scared—
scared people ain't scared of him no more.
Kids don't think twice about cutting across your lawn,
carving initials in your tree.
Yeah, they know he still got his musket
and missiles and Bible in the attic (they know
'cause you tell them in school—say
my daddy
will bomb your ass back to glass—not knowing
exactly what that means), but you know
like they do, he ain't really hit nothing
since World War II.

The neighbors laugh at the Terror-proof™ fence
he put up around the front yard—
you see old man Sam's house, they say,
just who does he think he is
putting the post side out?
He don't know
that when you put up a fence,
you supposed to take the ugly side.

In the Adjacent Days
(CIRCA 2001)

We do not want to write
this—to touch. It
is still wet, still burning.

We do not want to smear paint
and ash / blood and charcoal
on our hours of escape,

our humbled peace. The moon
unable to decide on a color, reflecting
the light of so many stars—

pale, yellowed white, blue, brazen.
We reflect on ourselves, our eyes
not opened but removed

and thrown back at us. We do not-want
to right this, pens tensed to play
prophet of what cannot happen.

Nuclear Winter: A Solstice

calamity makes cousins of us all
—Saul Stacey Williams

We few have been keeping busy
stitching together epiphanies
and plucking the feathers
off the dead phoenix in the backyard.
Together, the pieces make down comforters
for this new type of cold we face.
We're all niggers now—
our blackened limbs huddled
under these calico canons of sorts.

The sky is ashen, choking
as if god took a toke and released
all the Armageddon in his lungs.
I'm used to living in the dark. I feel
I should feel something for those
accustomed to the light. But
they must learn what is living benighted
by something so much bigger than your self.
Time to realize time is dead, history
decimated—the playing fields
finally eclipsed even.

Tidying Up

As children,
our grandmothers cleaned
other people's houses.
Sunday mornings,
their work follows us home.

We find loose purpose
under history's seat cushions—

Indian-head
pennies and frays
from linen shirts,
the toll for this time line.

Old Ways

FOR MS. ANNA

Saturday
night, sober. Matriarch
dead passed Easter
Sunday. The message,
lost,
finds me tonight. Grief retroactive
pounces.
I grab a lock
to fend it off—pull a curl taut.
Close eyes, close scissors/
slicing to make amends
and make
a mend.
Amputated hair
recoils,
rigor mortis—closing
like an envelope
blown to wind, no return
addressed.

My cousin's fiancé
by way of Lesotho,
taught me
this ritual: death, shed
hair
not water.
    It was the sea
that brought us our pain
in the first place.

For the Returning

We are a poet
who decomposes
what the world grows

and grows
from what the world
decomposes.

———————

Ancestors,
there is more
than a sea
between
us.

Your story waits, swelling,
taking shape
like a wave
craving to reclaim
the sand.

+ + +